AMERICAN ANTIQUARIAN SOCIETY

Book Culture in Post-Revolutionary Virginia

BY

JOSEPH F. KETT AND
PATRICIA A. McCLUNG

REPRINTED
FROM THE PROCEEDINGS
OF THE AMERICAN ANTIQUARIAN SOCIETY
VOLUME 94 · PART 1
APRIL 1984

Worcester, Massachusetts   1984   Published by the Society

Book Culture in
Post-Revolutionary Virginia

JOSEPH F. KETT and PATRICIA A. McCLUNG

I

As long as American intellectual history is conceived of as the study of successive systems of ideas from Puritanism to the present, most historians can agree on its major chronological divisions. For example, all concede that the major statements of American Transcendentalism appeared between 1836 and 1840 and that Transcendentalism succeeded Puritanism and preceded Darwinism. But there is another kind of intellectual history, the history of the process by which ideas and knowledge are diffused. Practitioners of this kind of intellectual history find it much more difficult to agree on chronological divisions than do their counterparts who study formal systems of ideas. While not questioning the publication date of Emerson's *Nature*, historians of the diffusion of knowledge are apt to point out that Emerson did not reach a popular audience until well after 1840, and then primarily as a lyceum lecturer; moreover, they note that cheap paperback editions of his books were not available until the late nineteenth century, indeed until after the conflagration over Darwinism had died down. Such historians might suggest, somewhat perversely, that in a sense Darwinism preceded Transcendentalism.

Nothing better illustrates the lack of consensus on dating the diffusion of ideas than a glance at some of the works on the history of the reading public. Louis B. Wright, for example, has pointed to the late sixteenth and early seventeenth centuries as a time marked by a notable increase in the size of the reading public in England.[1] Focusing on the narrower issue of literacy, David Cressy sees a much more gradual shift between the fifteenth and nineteenth centuries from restricted to mass literacy.[2] Still others argue that the democratization of the reading public began in earnest only during the eighteenth century. Lawrence Cremin portrays the rise of newspapers in eighteenth-century America as evidence of a growth of 'liberating literacy,' a kind of literacy marked by the fusion of technical competence in reading and an expanding need and desire to read.[3] Yet Cremin must contend on one side with the argument of Samuel Eliot Morison, who found that both literacy and love of books were widespread in seventeenth-century New England, and on the other with the different views offered by Robert Weir and Kenneth Lockridge.[4] Weir finds that the distribution of newspapers in the South at the time of the Revolution was sluggish and their format unappetizing. Lockridge's study of signatures on wills leaves him unconvinced of Morison's portrait of near-universal colonial literacy.

Not surprisingly, there is no consensus on the definition of

[1] Louis B. Wright, *Middle-Class Culture in Elizabethan England* (Chapel Hill, 1935), pp. 117–18.

[2] David Cressy, *Literacy and the Social Order: Reading and Writing in Tudor and Stuart England* (Cambridge, Eng., 1980), p. 175.

[3] Lawrence Cremin, *American Education: The Colonial Experience, 1607–1783* (New York, 1970), pp. 548–49.

[4] Samuel E. Morison, *The Puritan Pronaos: Studies in the Intellectual Life of New England in the Seventeenth Century* (New York, 1936), p. 138; Kenneth A. Lockridge, *Literacy in Colonial New England: An Inquiry into the Social Context of Literacy in the Early Modern West* (New York, 1974), p. 78. Ross W. Beales, Jr., suggests that Lockridge's data for New England needs upward revision. See Beales, 'Studying Literacy at the Community Level: A Research Note,' *Journal of Interdisciplinary History* 9(1978):93–102. In a study of townships in the Upper Connecticut Valley, William J. Gilmore has found near universal male literacy and very high levels of female literacy (eightieth percentile and up) between 1760 and 1830. See William J. Gilmore, 'Elementary Literacy on the Eve of the Industrial Revolution: Trends in Rural New England, 1760–1830,' *Proceedings of the American Antiquarian Society* 92(1982):87–171. Robert Weir, 'The Role of the Newspaper Press in the Southern Colonies on the Eve of the Revolution: An Interpretation,' in Bernard Bailyn and John B. Hench, eds., *The Press and the American Revolution* (Worcester, 1980), pp. 132–35. See also Donald H. Stewart, *The Opposition Press of the Federalist Period* (Albany, N.Y., 1969), p. 14.

the period when reading became widely diffused. Several historians such as Louis James and Richard D. Altick (for Britain) and Michael Schudson (for America) have contended that a mass reading public did not emerge until after 1830.[5] Yet other scholars have identified the critical period for reading as the years between 1780 and 1830. Maurice J. Quinlan estimated in 1941 that, while the population of England and Wales doubled during this period, the number of readers quintupled. In a similar vein, Q. D. Leavis has insisted that the process which saw Mrs. Radcliffe and Charlotte Smith displace Smollett and Fielding at the end of the eighteenth century coincided with the emergence of a mass, and intellectually addled, reading public.[6] For America, Gordon S. Wood has portrayed a 'democratization of mind' as a byproduct of the American Revolution, the result of a gradual recognition by eighteenth-century gentlemen that to sustain their positions of social leadership they would have both to address and to ingratiate themselves with a popular audience.[7] David D. Hall sees a shift during the same period not only toward greater accessibility of books but toward a less reverential, more pragmatic style of reading.[8]

Within this larger debate about the timing of the rise of print culture, a subsidiary debate has focused on the colonial

[5] Louis James, *Fiction for the Working Man, 1830–1850: A Study of the Literature Produced by the Working Class in Early Victorian Urban England* (London, 1963) p. 12; Richard D. Altick, *The English Common Reader: A Social History of the Mass Reading Public, 1800–1900* (Chicago, 1957), chaps. 6–9; Michael Schudson, *Discovering the News: A Social History of American Newspapers* (New York, 1978), chap. 1. Both James and Altick emphasize the emerging working-class quest for self-improvement. See also Thomas Laqueur, 'The Cultural Origins of Popular Literacy in England, 1500–1850,' *Oxford Review of Education*, vol. 2, no. 3(1976):255–75.

[6] M. J. Quinlan, *Victorian Prelude: A History of English Manners, 1700–1830* (New York, 1941), pp. 160–61; Q. D. Leavis, *Fiction and the Reading Public* (London, 1968), pp. 134, 157.

[7] Gordon S. Wood, 'The Democratization of Mind in the American Revolution,' in Robert Horwitz, ed., *The Moral Foundations of the American Republic* (Charlottesville, Va., 1977), pp. 102–28.

[8] David D. Hall, 'The Uses of Literacy in New England, 1600–1850,' in William L. Joyce, David D. Hall, Richard D. Brown, and John B. Hench, eds., *Printing and Society in Early America* (Worcester, 1983), pp. 1–47, esp. p. 23.

South. On one side, we have the testimony of Carl Bridenbaugh that Thomas Jefferson and James Madison were exceptional figures within the Chesapeake society for, by and
large, 'the denizens of the Chesapeake country were not a
reading people.' Even within the gentry, Bridenbaugh noted,
bookishness was exceptional: 'literary achievement is not to
be expected from an aristocracy whose members are concerned
with politics and the extroverted life of a rural people.'[9] More
recently, Rhys Isaac has described colonial Virginia as a place
where private libraries were small and the written word had
only marginal impact on most people.[10] Where Bridenbaugh
based his conclusion on an a priori deduction from his assump-
tion of the type of behavior appropriate to a rural, extroverted
people, Isaac could draw on Lockridge's evidence that literacy
in Virginia was significantly lower than in New England. Specifically, Lockridge surmised that in mid-eighteenth century
Virginia half of the middle and lower class could not sign their
names and perhaps a third of all males could neither read nor
write. In contrast, literacy in New England was approaching
90 percent at this time.[11] Yet this picture of the colonial South
as a desert of literary culture has not gone unchallenged. Scholars from Louis B. Wright to Richard Beale Davis have tried
to write what amounts to compensatory history by arguing
that Virginians were cultured as well as gracious and that literary interests were widespread in the colonial South.[12]

[9] Carl B. Bridenbaugh, *Myths and Realities: Societies of the Colonial South* (Baton Rouge, 1952), pp. 39–43.

[10] Rhys Isaac, 'Books and the Social Authority of Learning: The Case of Mid-Eighteenth Century Virginia,' in Joyce et al., *Printing and Society in Early America*, pp. 230–31. See also Isaac, *The Transformation of Virginia, 1740–1790* (Chapel Hill, 1982), chap. 6, and his 'Dramatizing the Ideology of the Revolution: Popular Mobilization in Virginia, 1774–1776,' *William and Mary Quarterly*, 3d ser. 33(1976):357–85, esp. p. 359.

[11] Lockridge, *Literacy in Colonial New England*, p. 78. For the difficulties encountered by an aspiring youth of humble origins in obtaining even a single book in eighteenth-century Virginia see Devereux Jarratt, *The Life of the Rev. Devereux Jarratt, Rector of Bath Parish, Dinwiddie County, Virginia* (Baltimore, 1806), pp. 24–40.

[12] Louis B. Wright, *First Gentlemen of Virginia: Intellectual Qualities of the Early Virginia Ruling Class* (San Marino, Calif., 1940), chap. 5; Richard Beale Davis, *Intellectual Life in the Colonial South*, 3 vols. (Knoxville, Tenn., 1978), 2:499, passim.

This lack of consensus about the scope of print culture in the colonial South has reflected the loose methodology of some contributors to the debate, the tendency, for example, to reconstruct book ownership from the contents of published inventories of estates (which are biased toward wealth and book ownership) or to rely on analysis of the titles of large libraries. The latter approach, while telling us the kind of books people owned, reveals nothing about the extent of book ownership.

Of course, loose methodology has not been a universal characteristic of the debate, but even where the methodology has been rigorous, historians have tended to assume that terms like the 'democratization of knowledge' or the 'emergence of a mass reading public' were descriptive of much of the nation during the nineteenth century, and were movements that swept region after region within a fairly compressed period of time. The declining price of books and the rapid spread of newspapers all lend plausibility to this view, as does the testimony of contemporaries. Speaking before Harvard's chapter of Phi Beta Kappa in 1826, Joseph Story proclaimed that the 'general diffusion of knowledge' was a 'leading characteristic of the times,' that his was 'emphatically an age of reading.'[13] During the same decade, Josiah Holbrook, the Connecticut educational reformer and popularizer of education for adults, expressed his conviction that lyceums would soon spread throughout the nation and indeed encircle the globe. Others affirmed that the 'universal diffusion of education' in America had created 'a great middling class of readers' without parallel elsewhere, that the means of gratifying literary taste were 'within the reach of almost every farmer.'[14]

Although earnest, these professions were neither accurate nor altogether disinterested. Any number of studies by librarians and sociologists during the Progressive Era demonstrated

[13] Joseph Story, 'The Characteristics of the Age,' in William W. Story, ed., *The Miscellaneous Writings of Joseph Story* (Boston, 1852), pp. 344–45.

[14] 'Increase in Book Business,' *Frank Leslie's Illustrated Weekly*, December 29, 1855, p. 38; see also Grace Landrum, 'Notes on the Reading of the Old South,' *American Literature* 3(1931):60–76.

the lack of accuracy of these forecasts, for as late as the first quarter of the twentieth century, large parts of the United States still lacked adequate access to books, periodicals, and libraries.[15] The inaccurate forecasting of Story and his contemporaries reflected a bias that historians have often ignored. Story and others used the phrase 'diffusion of knowledge' both descriptively and normatively. They believed not only that a progressive spread of knowledge through books, periodicals, and newspapers was occurring but *had* to occur if republican institutions were to thrive.

Agencies like lyceums, mechanics' institutes, popular self-culture societies, and popular lectures were devices by which gentlemen like Story could address a popular audience in a democratic age and win public respect not only for learning but for attendant cultural values like sobriety and self-discipline. It was tempting for promoters of these institutions to view the universal diffusion of knowledge as imminent, progressive, and inevitable. As a corollary, they rarely considered the possibility that differences between regions or between towns and rural areas within a region or between classes might prove to be profound and enduring. Rather, conservative politicians like the Whig governor of Massachusetts Edward Everett, who rivalled Story in his belief that the diffusion of knowledge was imminent, seized upon every sign of learning among the humble to drive home their point. It was Everett, for example, who discovered Elihu Burritt, 'the learned blacksmith,' who taught himself over twenty languages. Everett not only gave speeches on Burritt but introduced him to the Harvard faculty. Indeed, Burritt was the ideal Whig artisan, as self-effacing as he was self-improving, as scornful of strikes and agitation as he was enamored of learning. Nor did these advocates of the diffusion of knowledge attend much to the

---

[15] See, for example, Louis R. Wilson, *The Geography of Reading: A Study of the Distribution and Status of Libraries in the United States* (Chicago, 1938), pp. 102, 107, and passim. William S. Gray and Ruth Monroe, *The Reading Interests and Habits of Adults: A Preliminary Report* (New York, 1929), pp. 14, 18, 33.

possibility of distinctions between public education, literacy, and an improvement in literary taste. In their view, schools produced literate citizens who would develop a desire to read better books and to become sturdy citizens of the republic. In sum, their conviction that the diffusion of knowledge through the printed word would usher in a new age was not only a description of some tangible currents in their society but an ideological stance.[16]

To note this is to raise questions not only about the timing of the revolution in print but about its nature. Much of the evidence that a revolution in print (whether leading to a democratization of knowledge or the emergence of a mass reading public) occurred between the mid-eighteenth and mid-nineteenth centuries comes from the Northeast, particularly New England and cities like Boston and New York. Those who have studied the Northeast have never claimed that the patterns they have identified were typical of the nation as a whole; rather, they have assumed that the rest of the country took a few decades to catch up with the Northeast. Yet one can pose an alternative hypothesis, that during the nineteenth century it was actually the 'rest of the country' that set the standard and that it was the northeastern cities or New England towns that consistently deviated from this standard. The truth is that we do not know very much about the state of print culture nationally during the nineteenth century, certainly not enough to be

---

[16] The moral as well as intellectual goals of lyceums can be glimpsed in Josiah Holbrook, *The American Lyceum, or Society for the Improvement of Schools and Diffusion of Useful Knowledge* (Boston, 1829). Holbrook advanced the ideal of popularizing useful knowledge as an alternative to militia musters, dancing schools, grog shops, and conspicuous consumption. Ian Tyrrell has underscored the close links between lyceums and the temperance movement in *Sobering Up: From Temperance to Prohibition in Antebellum America, 1800–1860* (Westport, Conn., 1979), chap. 4. For the relationship between Everett and Burritt, see Peter Tolis, *Elihu Burritt: Crusader for Brotherhood* (Hamden, Conn., 1968), pp. 19–21. The idea that the triumph of popular knowledge, industrial progress, and temperance was imminent ran through the many addresses that Everett delivered before mechanics' lyceums during the 1830s and 1840s; see Edward Everett, 'A Discourse on the Importance to Practical Men of Scientific Knowledge and on Encouragement to its Pursuit,' in Edward Everett, *Orations and Speeches on Various Occasions* (Boston, 1836), pp. 231–64.

able to pronounce one or other section typical or a harbinger
of things to come. Indeed the concept of a 'section' is probably
too broad to be of much help to us in understanding what the
centers of print culture were during the nineteenth century.
Not only might two states in the same region have displayed
different characteristics, but even within a state there may have
been pronounced regional differences.[17]

Critical to our argument is a distinction between the reading
of books and other types of print. The newspaper was to become the most popular form of printed matter during the nineteenth century and it remains so, but there is evidence that the
proportion of readers of books has not risen correspondingly
with the growing popularity of other types of print. In 1978,
for example, the Book Industry Study Group commissioned
the firm of Yankelovich, Skelly, and White to survey the reading habits of Americans. The resulting study, based on hour-
long interviews with a representative sample of 1,450 adults
sixteen and over in 165 cities, revealed that 45 percent of the
population had not read a single book in the six months preceding the interview. While 94 percent of the population had
read either books, magazines, or newspapers in the period, the
study concluded that nearly half of the population were 'non-
book readers.' Further, of the book readers (the 55 percent of
the population who had read a book in the preceding six
months), 24 percent had read only one to three books. In addition, it is likely that the survey actually overstated the extent of book reading in American society in 1978.[18] In a dis-
cussion of the survey, Alexander Hoffman of Doubleday and
Company noted that his firm's experience with surveys had
led it to abandon them as tools of market research, for people
'constantly overstate by somewhat more than 100 percent'

[17] Although this observation is a commonplace among political historians, cultural
historians generally have not paid much attention to its implications. See, however,
Raymond Gastil, *Cultural Regions of the United States* (Seattle, 1975), pp. 174–204.

[18] John Y. Cole and Carol S. Gold, eds., *Reading in America, 1978* (Washington,
1979), pp. 62–66.

their reading habits. For example, while 16 percent of the adult population claimed that they belonged to book clubs, Hoffman noted that the actual figure was less than half that.[19]

Not allowed the luxury of interviewing our subjects, we have no way of knowing how many, if any, read a book every six months. But we have found a large class of non-owners along with a significant minority of substantial owners, a conclusion consistent not only with the findings of the BISG survey but also with similar surveys earlier in this century and with studies of the users of public libraries during the twentieth century, which have shown that a small class of heavy users actually accounts for most of the circulation of libraries.[20]

[19] Ibid., pp. 75–76.

[20] Scattered studies of twentieth-century communities as well as some surveys of twentieth-century opinion tend to support the BISG conclusions. In the 1920s, for example, James L. Hypes found that slightly fewer than two books a year were read in the average 'American' household in a rural New England town. The largest single category of books owned in such a town consisted of works of fiction, followed by religious works. Ninety-one percent of all books in the 'American' homes fell into these two categories. Hypes also surveyed the reading patterns in Polish, German, and Jewish households. The Jews surpassed all the other households, although not by much. In the average Jewish household, slightly fewer than three books a year were read. See Hypes, *Social Participation in a Rural New England Town* (Teachers College Contributions to Education, #258, New York, 1927), pp. 89–90. Other studies give a similar picture. Bernard Berelson noted in 1957 that about half of the adult population in the United States read a book every six months; 25–30 percent read a book a month; 6–8 percent read a book or more a week. See Berelson, 'Who Reads What Books and Why?' in Bernard Rosenberg and David M. White, *Mass Culture: The Popular Arts in America* (London, 1957), p. 120. In 1958, Adler and Mayer reported that in the United States only 17 percent of the adult population could be found reading a book at any given time. In Britain the figure was much higher, 55 percent. See Mortimer J. Adler and Milton Mayer, *The Revolution in Education* (Chicago, 1958), p. 118. There is evidence, in addition, that expenditures for books actually declined between 1920 and 1952. Drawing statistics from *Business Week*, Max Kaplan reported in 1960 that expenditures for books and maps comprised 7.1 percent of American expenditures for recreation in 1929, then went down to 6.4 percent in 1934, to 5.4 percent in 1952. See Kaplan, *Leisure in America: A Social Inquiry* (New York, 1960), p. 6. The best study of the users of libraries is Bernard Berelson, *The Library's Public* (New York, 1949). Analyzing users of the Free Public Library in Montclair, N.J., Berelson found that 'about three fourths of the books were borrowed by less than 5 percent of the adult population' (p. 102). Berelson describes the audience for books as the least extensive of any of the mass media audiences and notes that 'only 10 percent of the population accounts for fully 70 percent of the book reading, and 10 percent of the book readers themselves account for as much as 50 percent of the book reading' (p. 98).

II

In this essay we have sought to advance understanding of the history of the reading public by analyzing the distribution of books in post-Revolutionary Virginia. There is only one good way to measure the distribution of books, and that is by analyzing inventories of estates for evidence of ownership. This is the method that we have chosen. Our conclusions are based on an analysis of a large number of estates from Virginia during the late eighteenth and first half of the nineteenth century. Before turning to the conclusions, however, a few cautionary remarks are in order. Inventories are not without drawbacks. First, they do not record the estates of all decedents. According to Virginia law, every decedent, with or without a will, was to be probated in the jurisdiction where he owned a house or, if he did not own a house, where he died. But as several historians of other regions have noted, not everyone was probated. In a study of two Massachusetts counties between 1650 and 1720, Gloria Main found that the inventory coverage ranged from 25 percent to 60 percent of decedents.[21] Gary B. Nash has estimated that during the eighteenth century between 35 and 55 percent of Boston's males and between 14 and 23 percent of Philadelphia's males were inventoried.[22] Both Main and Nash based their estimates on a comparison of inventories and death records. Inasmuch as Virginia had no provisions for systematic death registration before 1853, we cannot be certain of the proportion of all decedents represented in our inventories. One group surely underrepresented were women, a reflection of laws restricting their ownership of property. In addition, inventories contain an age bias, for they

[21] Gloria B. Main, 'Probate Records as a Source for Early American History,' *William and Mary Quarterly*, 3d ser., 32(1975):98; see also Harold B. Gill, Jr., and George M. Curtis III, 'Virginia's Colonial Probate Policies and the Preconditions for Economic History,' *Virginia Magazine of History and Biography* 87(1979):71.

[22] Gary B. Nash, 'Urban Wealth and Poverty in Pre-Revolutionary America,' *Journal of Interdisciplinary History* 6(1976):548.

enumerate possessions at the ends of lives. Many books that appear in an inventory dated, for example, 1800, undoubtedly were acquired twenty or thirty years earlier. Inventories may also reveal a class bias. Naturally they omit slaves, who could not own personal property and were in fact a form of property. Even if they were free, the poor, especially the transient poor, were less likely to be inventoried than the wealthy.[23]

In addition to underrepresenting some groups, inventories probably undercounted some possessions. It is possible that they underrepresented pamphlets and periodicals, for such paperbound forms of print may have fallen apart before the inventory. They ignored newspapers, which, having no market value, were not inventoried even if kept. In addition, assessors may have missed books either because of carelessness or because sick people gave away books and other possessions in contemplation of death. Further, inventories often did not contain itemizations of the titles of books; rather, assessors frequently aggregated books under headings like 'a parcel of books' or 'one lot of books.' Finally, strictly speaking, inventories do not define reading tastes; we have no way of knowing whether an individual inherited books or purchased them, or whether he read them.

These qualifications are valid, but only up to a point, for there are ways to measure if not eliminate some of them. For example, the same city and county manuscript will books that contain inventories contain records of estate sales. Although the latter obviously did not record unsold items, we found a heartening degree of correspondence between inventories and estate sales. On the matter of book ownership, information

---

[23] Jackson T. Main estimated that during the colonial period inventories missed the bottom 10 percent of the white population. See his study *The Social Structure of Revolutionary America* (Princeton, 1965), p. 291. Main based this estimate partly on his conclusion that indentured servants were rarely inventoried. Since the number of indentured servants fell during the late eighteenth century, our inventories might be more representative of the entire free population than earlier inventories. On the other hand, we suspect that a lot of transients in port towns like Petersburg and Fredericksburg were not inventoried. Therefore, we are probably still missing the bottom tenth.

from inventories matched that from estate sales in all but six percent of our cases. Where there was a divergence, it was small. The inventory might not list any books, whereas the estate sale might list one or two. Although some individuals may have given away books in contemplation of death, we found several instances of relatives, including wives, purchasing books from a decedent's estate. Inasmuch as court-appointed assessors were often neighbors of the decedent and familiar with his possessions, it is unlikely that the practice of giving away books before death was widespread. One who owned many books would not escape notice; one who owned few would have little incentive to give them away. Further, as tables 2.0 and 2.1 indicate, our inventories represented a broad spectrum of the population, including the poor. In over a third of our inventories, personal estates were valued at less than $500. It is likely, moreover, that inventories reveal a good deal about reading tastes in the period. Contemporaries often wrote that individual books were treasured and read again and again.[24] Their observations are hardly surprising in view of the cost of books. Cynthia and Gregory Stiverson have calculated that even cheap primers sold for the equivalent of a day's wages of a carpenter during the 1750s (2s 6d). During the same decade, Tobias Smollett's multivolume *Complete History of England* sold for £9. Relative to purchasing power, books were far more expensive than today.[25] The expense of books made it likely that those purchased would be read. The correspondence between Mason Locke Weems, the peripatetic parson, historian, and hawker of books, and the Phila-

[24] See Jarratt, *Life*, pp. 39–40. Jarratt's account happens to be the only extensive record of the literary efforts of a poor youth in eighteenth-century Virginia. Testimony from other colonies, however, is similar. See William Plumer, Jr., *Life of William Plumer*, ed. A. P. Peabody (Boston, 1857), p. 20; Rena L. Vassar, ed., 'The Life or Biography of Silas Felton, Written by Himself,' *Proceedings of the American Antiquarian Society* 49(1959):172.

[25] Cynthia Z. Stiverson and Gregory A. Stiverson, 'The Colonial Book Trade: Availability and Affordability of Reading Material in Mid-Eighteenth Century Virginia,' in Joyce et al, *Printing and Society in Early America*, pp. 170–71.

delphia publisher Mathew Carey provides abundant evidence of a flourishing book market in Virginia during the early Republic.[26] Weems frequently paused in his lamentations of Carey's surly treatment of him to beg for more copies of spellers, of Guthrie's *A New System of Modern Geography*, of Watson's *Reply to Paine*, and of Goldsmith's *Animated Nature*, all works that we found in abundance in the inventories.[27]

Our study is based on nearly 2,400 inventories drawn from two towns (Petersburg and Fredericksburg) and five counties (Alleghany, Botetourt, Charles City, Fairfax, and Lunenburg). The bulk of our inventories fall into the period between 1790 and 1830, during which many historians have detected the emergence of a mass reading public. But we have examined all extant inventories in Petersburg from 1784 to 1859, Fredericksburg from 1782 to 1840, Alleghany from 1822 to 1874, Charles City from 1782 to 1845, Fairfax and Lunenburg from 1780 to 1816, and Botetourt from 1770 to 1780, 1811 to 1815, 1826 to 1830, 1836 to 1840, 1846 to 1850, and 1856 to 1861. To foreshadow a point made in the conclusion, these locations, taken collectively, do not constitute a microcosm of Virginia's population during the late eighteenth or first half of the nineteenth century. They were selected in part to provide geographical coverage of several of the state's major regions: Northern Neck (Fairfax), Southside (Lunenburg), Tidewater (Charles City), Valley (Botetourt), and trans-Valley (Alleghany). They were also selected because Petersburg and Fredericksburg were incorporated towns that kept their records separate from those of surrounding counties, which makes it possible to test the hypothesis that the key differences were less between counties in different areas than between towns and counties. For this purpose, the inventories of the two towns served very well, but the reader should be fore-

---

[26] Emily E. F. Skeel, *Mason Locke Weems: His Works and Ways,* 3 vols. (New York, 1929), vols. 2, 3.

[27] Ibid., 2:57, 59, 100–105.

warned that the great majority of Virginians did not live in towns like Petersburg and Fredericksburg.[28]

Although we have found abundant evidence that intellectual culture flourished in the post-Revolutionary South, our analysis of unpublished inventories helps to define the limits of that culture. Almost half of the inventories (1,192 out of 2,386) failed to record a single book or periodical. This 50 percent average concealed a range of book ownership from as low as 31.7 percent in Charles City County to as high as 61.6 percent in Lunenburg, but nowhere else did even 55 percent of the inventories reveal books or periodicals; indeed, in Petersburg, Charles City, and Botetourt, the proportion of owners of books or periodicals was below half. Furthermore, contrary to our initial expectations, the proportion of owners did not rise during the nineteenth century. In Petersburg, for example, a higher proportion of estates inventoried before 1830 contained books or periodicals than of those inventoried after 1830. (See tables 1.0, 1.1, 1.2, and 3.0.) In addition, if we put aside Charles City County, the counties actually exhibited higher rates of book ownership than the cities, which is again contrary to what one might expect.

Surprising as they may be, these conclusions are in some ways misleading, for they fail to consider book ownership among free blacks. Unlike slaves, free blacks could be inven-

---

[28] Ours is not the first effort to use probate records to gain insight into print culture in the Old South. Some previous studies have relied on published inventories. See, for example, George Smart, 'Private Libraries in Colonial Virginia,' *American Literature* 10(1938):24–52; Louis B. Wright, 'The Gentleman's Library in Early Virginia,' *Huntington Library Quarterly* 1(1937):3–61. While they contain valuable insights, such studies are obviously biased toward large libraries. Others have used unpublished inventories, but without much analysis of the contents of libraries. See, for example, Main, *The Social Structure of Revolutionary America*, pp. 254–58 and Freeman H. Hart, *The Valley of Virginia in the American Revolution* (Chapel Hill, 1942), p. 167. (Neither of these books, it should be added, is primarily concerned with the scope of print culture, and hence their omissions are understandable.) One of the most exhaustive studies of inventories was carried out in the 1940s by Joseph T. Wheeler. In his essay 'Literary Culture in Eighteenth-Century Maryland, 1700–1776,' *Maryland Historical Magazine* 38(1943):273–76, Wheeler studied some 4,000 inventories, but he did not identify the universe from which he selected his inventories, and at one point he implied that he selected 'specific lawyers, clergymen, doctors, merchants and planters' (p. 276).

toried, but, poor and often illiterate, they were unlikely to own books.[29] Petersburg, Fredericksburg, and Charles City County all contained a sizable number of free blacks during the first half of the nineteenth century. In 1810, free blacks comprised 31.2 percent of the free population of Petersburg and 21.7 percent of that of Fredericksburg. By 1830, free blacks comprised 37.2 percent of the free population of Petersburg and 17.5 percent of that of Fredericksburg. Free blacks formed 17.9 percent of the free population of Charles City in 1810 and 30.4 percent in 1830. In the other counties, free blacks were never more than 8 percent of the free population.

Because free blacks comprised so high a percentage of the free population of Petersburg and Charles City County during the antebellum period (30 percent or more in 1830), it is probable that the modest decline in the proportion of book owners in Petersburg after 1830, and the sharp slump in Charles City County's proportion after 1800, reflects a change in the population eligible to be inventoried rather than a real change in the proportion of the population that owned books. Would the percentages in table 3.0 change significantly if we eliminated free blacks? Although inventories do not reveal race, it is possible to answer this question indirectly by eliminating all estates valued at less than $100. We were able to identify a dozen individuals in Petersburg as free blacks; none owned books and virtually all had estates under $100. As table 2.2 indicates, individuals with such small estates were notably less likely than others to own books. While the procedure of eliminating estates of less than $100 is defensible, it introduces a countervailing bias, for some of these small estates were undoubtedly those of poor whites rather than free blacks. The reader should bear in mind, therefore, that the truth lies somewhere between the percentages in table 3.0 and what follows.

---

[29] With the help of another scholar, Suzanne D. Lebsock, we were able to identify a dozen men and women in Petersburg as free blacks, although the actual number of free blacks in our inventories was certainly much larger. Of the dozen, none owned any books.

If we eliminate estates of less than $100, the percentages of book owners in Petersburg and Charles City County change. Before 1801, the proportion of book owners in Petersburg was 53.3 percent, that for Charles City County 47.3 percent. For Petersburg between 1831 and 1859, and for Charles City County between 1831 and 1845, the respective proportions were 42.3 percent and 25.4 percent. By eliminating estates under $100, the proportion of book owners in Petersburg before 1801 becomes 50.1 percent, while that for Charles City County stays the same (since there were no such estates), 47.3 percent. For the period after 1830, the proportions change to 43.1 percent and 26.4 percent respectively. In other words, with respect merely to the proportion of people who owned books, the bias introduced by the presence of so many free blacks in these two locations was very slight.

Inasmuch as free blacks formed only a negligible proportion of the free population in Alleghany, Botetourt, Fairfax, and Lunenburg, the modest rates of ownership of books in these places certainly reflected either the indifference of many whites to print culture or their inability to acquire books. It is likely that similar forces were at work among most whites in Charles City County, and that the effect there of the high proportion of free blacks was to depress slightly the county's proportion of book owners. In Petersburg and Fredericksburg, however, we suspect that the presence of so many free blacks (nearly 40 percent of Petersburg's population in 1830) concealed the existence of an extremely lively culture of books. This suspicion gains support if one looks not at the fact of ownership but at the size of private libraries. Since the majority of inventories did not contain itemizations of titles, it became necessary to identify monetary equivalents to books. The average valuation of a book was thirty cents. Using this figure, we found that in Petersburg 37.4 percent of all book owners owned either twenty or more books or books evaluated at six dollars or more. The comparable figure for Fredericksburg was 51.5 percent. As table 4.0 indicates, the closest county was Fairfax, with 30.8 percent. Since some books were valued at several dollars and others at less than ten cents, there are risks in extrapolating from an average of thirty cents. To provide another perspective, tables 4.1 and 4.2 compare all locations on the sole basis of the monetary value of books. Residents of Petersburg and Fredericksburg were two to three times more likely than county residents to own books valued at $20 or more and exactly three times likelier to own books valued at $50 or more.

Merely to note these differences in the monetary value of books fails to convey the magnitude of many of the urban private libraries in our survey. We are talking about individuals who owned fifty, one hundred, even two hundred or three hundred books, individuals who usually had, at most, local reputations, and often no more than moderately large estates of a few thousand dollars. Our findings are relevant to an issue often neglected by historians of reading in America who write of a revolutionary democratization of print culture, argue about its timing, but do not tell us exactly what the revolution has amounted to. It is seductively tempting to suppose that, once the revolution was underway, each successive generation of Americans could count a higher proportion of its members as readers. Yet our evidence fails to indicate a growth of either the proportion of individuals who owned books or of the size of their book holdings after 1830. It is likely that significant upward changes occurred in the incidence of book ownership in America between the seventeenth and eighteenth centuries. Data for Massachusetts analyzed by Samuel Eliot Morison and Jackson T. Main indicates this, and common sense suggests that the same must have been true in Virginia; for one can scarcely imagine an environment less conducive to the cultivation of books than that of the seventeenth-century Chesapeake.[30] But, once established, patterns of book ownership and

[30] On the differences between seventeenth- and eighteenth-century Massachusetts, compare Morison, *Puritan Pronaos*, p. 138 and Main, *Social Structure of Revolutionary America*, p. 254.

reading have probably been more enduring than is often recognized.

Some changes in the consumption of books undoubtedly have occurred since the early or mid-nineteenth century, but the changes have probably come more in the composition than in the proportion of serious book readers. It is likely, for example, that women form a significantly greater part of the serious reading public than in the past. It is certain that the spread of public libraries, a movement that did did not really affect the South until after 1900, has made books more available in rural areas. In contrast, we found, as noted, striking differences in book ownership between urban and rural areas. Specifically, our evidence indicates that, while rural residents were as likely as inhabitants of cities to own books, they were much less likely to own substantial numbers of books. Our evidence is quantitative, but the difference between the towns and the country was, in essence, qualitative. In planning Fredericksburg's first book store (which opened in 1796), Lancelot Mullin wrote to his distributor, Philadelphia's Mathew Carey, that Fredericksburg was 'extremely well adapted' for such an enterprise because its people were 'Generally Rich, Well Educated, & fond of the study of literature.'[31] Quantitative measures help to explain this fondness for the study of literature but in the final analysis do not fully account for it.

Among the quantifiable differences between the towns and counties are those of literacy, personal wealth, and occupations. Each merits consideration, but the reader should be forewarned that it is risky to extract from any or all of them a quality such as fondness for literature. Indeed, there is no good way to measure literacy. Historians have usually based estimates of literacy on the proportion of wills bearing signatures rather than marks, a method that allows some useful comparisons between different regions at the same time or between

[31] Skeel, *Weems*, 2:37.

the same region at different times but one that leaves us in the dark about why some people became avid readers while others did not. Since we have not made a study of signatures on wills (for various reasons, a much more laborious task than it might seem), we are forced back on the federal census of 1840, which contained a question about the proportion of white persons unable to 'read and write.' The question virtually invited qualitative judgments, but, for what it is worth, the proportion of white persons in Petersburg and Fredericksburg unable to 'read and write' was virtually the same as that for the counties.

Nor do disparities in personal wealth account for the differences in book ownership between the towns and the counties. As tables 2.1 and 2.2 indicate, those with estates valued at less than $100 were significantly less likely than others to own books, but the differences between the towns and the counties in the distribution of personal wealth were slight. Further, in one of the towns, Petersburg, we found several instances of individuals with small estates but with substantial book holdings. Nearly 15 percent of Petersburg estates evaluated at less than $500 and over 20 percent of those evaluated at less than $1,000 contained books valued at $50 or more. The comparable percentages in Fredericksburg were 6.0 and 7.0. In the five counties they were negligible. The frequency of small estates with substantial holdings in books in Petersburg (and to a lesser extent in Fredericksburg) reinforces our contention that differences in wealth did not account for the difference between the size of libraries in the towns and in the counties.

The third measurable difference between the towns and the counties was the distribution of occupations. Historians of literacy such as Kenneth Lockridge and David Cressy have found a strong correlation between literacy and occupation. Reacting against older views that traced the spread of literacy to the diffusion of formal education, Lockridge and Cressy have documented the connection between the acquisition of an ability to read and the economic value of reading. As Cressy puts it,

'People involved in trade, specialized manufacturing, and farming for the market increasingly found themselves confronted by print or script, and more of them maintained written records of their transactions. In a world growing more familiar with bills and reckonings, acquitances and memoranda, the ability to read such instruments could be turned to personal advantage, even if there was a specialist on hand to write them.'[32] Cressy's contention is restricted to literacy in early modern England, but a version of his argument has infiltrated some studies of book ownership in eighteenth-century America in the form of an argument that professional men were more likely to own books than merchants and merchants more likely to own books than farmers.[33]

Although there is a correlation between occupation and book ownership, efforts to explain the much higher incidence of large private libraries in towns by references to the distinctive features of urban occupations leave us skeptical. It is true that towns contained a higher proportion of professional men—ministers, physicians, lawyers, and schoolmasters—and that, whether situated in towns or countryside, professional men owned a lot of books. From various sources, we were able to identify two ministers, nine physicians, five lawyers, and four schoolmasters in Petersburg and Fredericksburg. For the counties, we found ten physicians, five lawyers, three ministers, and one teacher. Of these thirty-nine men, twenty-one had $50 or more in books; seventeen had $100 or more; nine had $200 or more. But the proportion or professional men in our survey was small, less than 2 percent of all the inventories. Further, even within the professional class there were differences between urban and rural libraries. The average value of the libraries of professional men in Petersburg and Fredericksburg was $191, while that of professional men in the five counties was $89.

Efforts to expand explanations of book ownership in terms

32 Cressy, *Literacy and the Social Order*, p. 11.
33 See, for example, Main, *Social Structure of Revolutionary America*, p. 11.

of occupational distribution encounter the problem that urban and rural occupations differed. The great majority of country dwellers engaged in agriculture; few residents of the towns did. Although urban merchants were more likely to own large numbers of books than farmers with comparable estates, we cannot conclude from this that something in the nature of being a merchant made a man an avid collector of books. A sizable number of urban merchants and proprietors (the latter category embracing innkeepers, grocers, etc.) did not own any books. In Petersburg, for example, we were able to identify sixty-eight men as merchants or proprietors; of these, twenty-seven did not own any books. This proportion of non-owners (39.7 percent) was lower than that for Petersburg in general (51.4 percent), but high enough to indicate that the mere fact that someone routinely dealt with writing in his business did not necessarily make him a substantial owner of books. What can be said is that town merchants and proprietors who owned books usually owned a lot more of them than did rural merchants and proprietors with books. The books of town merchant-proprietors had an average value per estate of $74, more than double the $34 for merchant-proprietor book owners in the five counties. Averages, of course, are often misleading. In this case, they understate the town advantage, for the county average was driven up by a single estate with $200 in books. No other county estate had as much as $50 in books. In contrast, the Petersburg inventories show eleven merchant-proprietors with books valued at $50 or more and seven valued at $100 or more. Similarly, the average valuation for books of town artisan owners was $14, that for county artisan owners $4. Only one of the ten men identified as rural artisan owners had more than $20 worth of books, and of the remaining nine none owned as much as $10. In contrast, of twenty-seven town artisan owners, eleven owned books valued at $10 or more and five $20 or more.[34]

---

[34] We are indebted to Suzanne D. Lebsock for graciously sharing with us her data on the occupations of Petersburg residents.

Quantifiable factors like wealth and occupation help to explain urban-rural differences, but not very much. Residents of Petersburg and Fredericksburg were more likely to be physicians or lawyers or schoolmasters, in other words to follow professions in which books were indispensable. But to comprehend fully the differences between the size of urban and rural libraries, we have to consider the sort of non-quantifiable differences that Lancelot Mullin hinted at when he described residents of Fredericksburg as fond of the study of literature. Mullin planned a book store not to create a demand for books but to meet an existing demand, one that predated establishment of cultural institutions like book stores, libraries, and schools and which grew out of the opportunities that life in towns provided for literary exchange between the like-minded. Petersburg, for example, was well-served by cultural institutions from the 1790s on. These included several book stores, a library association called the Speculative Society, formed in 1793 and incorporated two years later, an academy incorporated in 1794, and an apprentices' library launched during the 1820s. All of these institutions contributed to the diffusion of literary interests, but many of them had a transient existence. Both the Speculative Society and the academy, for example, were defunct by the mid-1830s. Their direct contributions to the spread of interest in literature were probably less important than the public activities of the men who created them. These were individuals like the printer William Prentis who started the town's first press and newspaper in 1786, the historian John W. Campbell, the Scottish merchant David Anderson who bequeathed most of his estate to the town for the education of poor white children, and the young men who formed a Thespian Society to give benefits for the academy. While urban booksellers like Mullin distributed books in rural areas, and while rural merchants often stocked books and hawkers like Weems travelled the countryside, rural areas lacked the stimulus to literary interests that such public testimonials by leading men to the value of literature and education provided.[35]

III

More important than the size of libraries are their contents. What kinds of books did people own, and what, if anything, did their possession say about popular intellectual culture? There are risks in generalizing about reading tastes on the basis of books listed in inventories. Not only did the latter include books that were inherited as well as those that were purchased, but even the purchase of books took place under conditions radically different from those of our own time.

One important difference lies in the prevalence of the subscription system during the late eighteenth and early nineteenth centuries. Based on surviving evidence from Mason Weems's itinerant bookselling, this system was the basis of the rural book trade and played a substantial role in the town trade as well. A book sold by subscription was one that had yet to be printed in America (or anywhere) or, if printed, was still in the publisher's warehouse. Because of the high cost of printing and deficiencies in methods of transportation, itinerant agents could not cart a publisher's entire stock in the hope of finding interested customers; hence both had to rely on the subscription system. Weems employed a variation of the

[35] On Petersburg's intellectual climate, see Edward A. Wyatt IV, 'Schools and Libraries in Petersburg, Virginia, Prior to 1861,' *Tyler's Quarterly Historical and Genealogical Magazine* 19(1937):65–78; James G. Scott ahd Edward A. Wyatt IV, *Petersburg's Story: A History* (Petersburg, Va., 1960), pp. 109, 112, 121. Petersburg had a large complement of Scottish merchants like Anderson, men who were usually well-educated and cosmopolitan. See Wyatt, 'Schools and Libraries,' pp. 69–70. On the influence of Scottish merchants in eighteenth-century Virginia see R. Walter Coakley, 'The Two James Hunters of Fredericksburg,' *Virginia Magazine of History and Biography* 56(1948):4–5. During the middle of the eighteenth century Fredericksburg was one of the few places in Virginia to which the Society for the Propagation of the Gospel in Foreign Parts (SPG) dispatched its religious books. See John Chamberlin Van Horne, ' "Pious Designs:" The American Correspondence of the Associates of Dr. Bray, 1731–1775,' 2 vols. (Ph.D. diss. University of Virginia, 1979), 2:937, 940. In contrast to the vigorous cultural life of these towns, large sections of the Virginia countryside remained culturally barren well into the nineteenth century. For a glimpse of conditions, see William F. Mugleston, ed., 'The Freedmen's Bureau and Reconstruction in Virginia: The Diary of Marcus Sterling Hopkins, a Union Officer,' *Virginia Magazine of History and Biography* 86(1978):50 and passim.

system. He deposited large quantities of books that Carey had consigned to him with printers and booksellers in the towns. He next secured testimonials from prominent citizens who had either heard about a book or perhaps had read a British edition. He then carried these testimonials from house to house to secure down payments. When enough down payments to ensure a profit had been obtained, Weems obtained books from his deposits. On receipt, the buyer paid in full.[36]

While cumbersome, the subscription system did allow a response to demand, and innumerable references in Weems's letters to Carey make it clear that popular literary preferences existed. These preferences were influenced by the same sort of social hierarchies that influenced most of the other elements of Virginia society, for they rested on the testimonials of prominent men. But they can be described, nevertheless, as preferences. Some books failed to gain subscribers. Others like Oliver Goldsmith's *An History of the Earth and Animated Nature* were (at least for Weems) spectacular and surprising successes.

The listings of books in inventories do permit generalizations about popular taste. The Bible was by far the most commonly itemized title in our inventories; it was, undoubtedly, the most popular book in America. It was listed in more than half of the itemized inventories in Fredericksburg, for example, and in almost three quarters of those in Lunenberg County. In fact, the Bible accounted for 25 percent of the entire list of itemized books in Lunenburg. Weems recognized the demand for Bibles; he often wrote to Carey begging for more copies for his 'Numerous and Clamerous' subscribers. 'Good old Book,' he apostrophied, 'I hope we shall live by you in this world and in the world to come.' Ann Stevenson of Fredericksburg, who died in 1830, lacked Weems's roguish wit, but

---

[36] For details of the methods Weems used in the subscription trade, see James Gilreath, 'Mason Weems, Mathew Carey and the Southern Booktrade, 1794–1810,' *Publishing History* 10(1981):31.

she willed a Bible to each of her relatives, viewing it as 'the best and richest donation I could possibly leave them.'[37]

Mere ownership of a Bible did not exclude secular tastes in literature, but we found that for all locations 70 percent of the books in small libraries (ten or fewer itemized titles) were religious. In Petersburg and Fredericksburg the proportion of religious books in small libraries was lower (50 percent), but small libraries in the counties were overwhelmingly religious in character. If a man owned only a few books, they were likely to be religious ones. The fact that small, itemized libraries were dominated by religious books leads us to suspect that the same was true of unitemized libraries valued at less than, say, six dollars. Bibles were often valued at five or six dollars or more. As Weems recognized, the demand was not just for Bibles but for elegant ones; men wanted 'one *Bible*, as one *Wife*, in their life times,' and wished 'to have *that one* of the best sort.'[38]

If we turn from these small libraries to a general classification of titles in all libraries, we get a different picture. To compile table 5.0 we used eighteen distinct categories of subjects. Two caveats are in order. First, although contemporaries at times classified their own libraries by subject, we suspect that none would have employed as many categories as we have included; and many would have found strange some of the categories, such as how-to-do-it books, which we have employed. Our categories reflect the curiosity of twentieth-century scholars rather than early nineteenth-century cosmologies. Second, we do not pretend that the table offers a snapshot of the Virginia 'mind,' for it reflects titles only in the 30 percent of libraries that were itemized. They were usually the larger libraries and were more likely to be found in the towns than in the counties. This much said, the table prompts us to offer a few general comments. Although religious titles comprised

[37] Skeel, *Weems*, 2:136. Fredericksburg Will Book, vol. C: 127.
[38] Skeel, *Weems*, 3:75.

the largest single category, they were, nonetheless, a minority of all titles. The preponderance of titles was secular and spread over a wide range of fields, from history and biography to novels, gazetteers, self-instructors, encyclopedias, and dictionaries. In general, we found that the proportion of secular titles grew after 1800 and that secular interests were more pronounced in the towns than in the counties.

Terms like 'secular' and 'religious' fail to convey much about the texture of literary culture. Within the sphere of religious books, it is important to note, for example, that works of practical piety—psalters, hymn books, collections of sermons, and prayer books—prevailed over books about theology. Within the field of theology, commentaries on the Bible were more common than polemical books. We found no polemical books that defended or attacked specific denominations, no signs, in other words, of internecine warfare among Christians. The most common polemical work, rather, was *An Apology for the Bible* by Richard Watson, Bishop of Llandaff, which was an attack on Paine's *The Age of Reason. Part the Second*. Weems warned Carey in 1798 never to send him copies of Paine without Watson's reply and preferred that Carey merely send Watson without Paine, lest the 'Lords spiritual here . . . tear me to pieces.'[39] But Weems's exhortation should not obscure the prevalence of piety over apologetics.

A practical motif also infused the secular books in Virginia inventories. In table 5.0, the most direct representation of this lies in the category of self-instructors or how-to books. This category includes manuals on how to cook, garden, survey roads, and farm, as well as advice on how to speak clearly, pilot a ship, and perform any number of other ordinary tasks. Several other categories in the same table also reflected, although less directly, the practical interests of Virginians. Dictionaries, grammars, arithmetics, and spellers were as com-

[39] Ibid., 2:107.

mon as self-instructors (see that category in table 5.0). To a lesser but still significant extent, we found books on law and collections of public documents, most often the statutes of Virginia (see categories in table 5.0). One would expect this in the estates of lawyers. What is interesting is that books about the law and collections of laws often appeared in the estates of physicians, merchants, and others.

In general, individuals who owned secular books in abundance were likely to own works on history, books of poetry, novels, and essays as well as self-instructors. Such individuals were clearly inclined to rely on books for pleasure as well as for immediately useful information. The degree of interest in history is particularly striking. To get a fair idea of the extent of that interest, one should add the great majority of titles aggregated in the category for Greece and Rome to those in the category of history, biography, and memoirs in table 5.0; roughly 80 percent of the books in the category on Greece and Rome were historical studies of the ancient world. The classical revival clearly affected more than architecture in Virginia, for we found a deep and enduring interest in ancient civilizations.

In contrast to this intense interest in history, we found surprisingly few novels. Naturally, with each passing decade, a few new authors appeared. The romances of Mrs. Radcliffe and Regina Maria Roche took their place alongside *Roderick Random*, *Humphrey Clinker*, *Peregrine Pickle*, *Tristram Shandy*, and *Tom Jones*. Not surprisingly, Sir Walter Scott was becoming popular by the 1820s and in time the author of *Waverly* was joined by Paulding, Cooper, Irving, and Bulwer-Lytton. The proportion of itemized libraries listing novels rose in Petersburg, for example, from 26 percent before 1801 to 43 percent after 1801. Yet even though the numbers of novels grew, such fiction, which comprised 3.2 percent of all titles before 1801, comprised only 6.9 percent of all titles between 1840 and 1860. Further, virtually none of our inventories listed an abundance of novels. The largest single repository of fiction was contained in an estate inventoried in Petersburg during the 1840s; yet even in this estate only 14 of over 150 titles were novels. Far more common were estates with as many as 30 to 50 or more titles which contained either no novels or merely a few. Within the category of belles-lettres (see table 5.0), books of poetry, Shakespeare, critical essays, and works like Blair's *Lectures on Rhetoric* were more common than novels.

Inasmuch as we usually associate the antebellum era with the rising appeal of fiction, the modest showing of novels in our inventories is surprising. One possible explanation is that this modest showing is itself fictitious, an artifact of defects in the source of our evidence. The possibility is worth considering. As noted, inventories often did not itemize titles, and hence certainly understated the number of novels that people actually possessed. But this was true of any kind of book. The fact remains that novels formed a modest proportion of all itemized titles. Inventories also underrepresented women, who, according to contemporaries, were becoming an avid class of novel readers during the early nineteenth century. But widows and spinsters were inventoried, and their estates contained even less fiction than those of men. Married women were not inventoried, but if they pre-deceased their husbands and owned fiction, the latter should have shown up in their husbands' estates. Finally, for some reason assessors were less likely to itemize titles in estates inventoried after 1840, the very period when one would expect novels acquired during the 1820s and 1830s to begin to show up. But even in the smaller universe of itemized libraries after 1840, fiction continued to play a minor role; the proportion of novels in estates inventoried after 1840 was only slightly higher than in those inventoried in the preceding three decades. As noted, in Petersburg between 1840 and 1860, 6.9 percent of the titles were novels; during the three decades before 1840, 5.3 percent were novels.

For these reasons, we conclude that the modest proportion of novels in our inventories is not a product of defects in the source but instead reflected the fact that Virginians owned less fiction than is often thought. There were of course, ways to read fiction without owning it. Newspapers, for example, sometimes serialized novels. This was a cheap way to read a novel, but also a cumbersome one, and it is difficult to understand why an individual who could afford to own many books and who had a craving for fiction would have been content to read serializations. It was also possible to obtain books from libraries. Both social and circulating libraries were common in eighteenth- and early nineteenth-century America, and while they flourished mainly in New England and the middle states, Virginia was not bereft of these 'public' (that is, open to the public) libraries. Because the social libraries were often incorporated, we know more about them, including the fact that they did not stock much fiction at all. That function was left to the circulating libraries, which were profit ventures often conducted by booksellers. Finally, if Virginians were getting their fiction from circulating libraries, one would expect to find quantities of it in the inventoried stock of booksellers. In fact, we found very little. In no case did novels constitute more than a small fraction of the inventories of booksellers.[40]

How, then, does one account for the discrepancy between this conclusion and the comments of contemporaries that a craze for fiction, stimulated by the novels of Sir Walter Scott and reinforced by those of Washington Irving and Fenimore Cooper, was sweeping the country after 1815? Although it is impossible to assess their relative importance, there are several possible answers. First, people may have desired to read

[40] The standard study of subscription or social libraries is Jesse Shera, *Foundations of the Public Library: The Origins of the Public Library Movement in New England, 1629–1855* (Chicago, 1949). Examples of these libraries in Virginia can be found in Joseph D. Eggleston, ed., 'The Minute Book of the Buffalo Circulating Library: Prince Edward County Virginia, 1803–18,' *Virginia Magazine of History and Biography* 49(1941):157–73. (Despite its title, this appears to have been a subscription library or joint-stock company rather than a proprietary venture library.) See also Charles W. Turner, 'The Franklin Society, 1800–1891,' *Virginia Magazine of History and Biography* 66(1958):432–47.

more fiction than they could obtain. The Virginia book market of the early nineteenth century contained a number of imperfections. One of Weems's most persistent laments was that Carey sent him too many unsaleable books such as abstruse theological tomes that he had no more chance of selling than fiddles at a Methodist meeting house, while neglecting to send him novels and other types of literature that he could sell with ease.[41] Second, unlike poetry and history, fiction was a controversial genre. Moralists argued that it bred false ideas of life and unfitted men and women (especially women) for their duties. In short, fiction was regarded as a vice. We know that contemporary moralists frequently engaged in hyperbole when describing other kinds of vice; it is possible that they did the same when confronting fiction. Further, there *was* a gradual growth of interest in fiction evidenced by estates inventoried after 1800 and especially after 1810; it was scarcely an explosion, but it did represent an upswing. The points to grasp, however, are that this interest was part of a gradual shift toward secular literature of all kinds, and that novels occupied a position subordinate to other kinds of secular literature.

Even when novels did begin to make their way into private libraries with increasing frequency, they did so without any fine sensitivity to shifts in the literary *Zeitgeist*. Unlike literary histories and university lecture courses in which new schools of literature displace the old, in libraries the new simply acquires a position on the shelf next to the old. Thus, while Scott entered in the 1820s and 1830s, Tobias Smollett and Laurence Sterne did not exit from private libraries. Different kinds of fiction remained available to each new generation of readers. By this measure of availability, indeed, Scott did not enjoy any special preeminence in libraries, even in those inventoried after 1820. Taking all locations over the entire period covered by our inventories, the novel most frequently

[41] Skeel, *Weems*, 3:102.

itemized was *Don Quixote*, followed by Smollett's *Adventures of Peregrine Pickle* and *Roderick Random*. Alain Le Sage's *Gil Blas*, another picaresque novel, the first parts of which appeared in France in 1715, followed closely. This ranking is a little misleading, however, for Cervantes and Le Sage were known only by the works cited. In contrast, we found several references to the 'Works' of Smollett, Sterne, and Scott, as well as individual references to *Peregrine Pickle*, *Roderick Random*, *Humphrey Clinker*, *Tristram Shandy*, *Waverley*, and *Rokeby*. If we add the collective to the individual references, Smollett, Sterne, and Scott were more frequently mentioned than Cervantes and Le Sage. Virginians were also familiar with Fielding, but more so with Smollett, who was not only a more prolific novelist but also the translator of *Don Quixote*, *Gil Blas*, and François Fénelon's *Adventures of Telemachus*, another early eighteenth-century French novel often found in Virginia libraries a century later. In cataloguing frequencies of mention, we are not trying to conduct a popularity contest through inventories, but to suggest that, while Virginians may have been acquiring or buttressing notions of chivalry and honor from Scott, they were simultaneously exposed to an older type of novel, the picaresque romance, which mocked chivalry and honor.[42]

[42] Robert B. Winans has used the catalogues issued by American booksellers to identify the twenty-four most 'popular' novels between 1750 and 1800. Many of the novels that appear on Winans's list of favorites appear also on ours, for example, *Don Quixote*, *The Vicar of Wakefield*, and *Humphrey Clinker*. On the other hand, some of the novels Winans identifies as popular rarely if ever appeared in our inventories. Examples include *The Sorrows of Werther* and *Robinson Crusoe*. We take this not as proof that such novels were unpopular—doubtless they were popular somewhere else—but that there were eccentricities in local markets. People only bought a book if a bookseller or colporteur had it for sale, and booksellers sold only what they could get from publishers like Carey. Winans makes an additional observation relevant to our conclusions when he notes that picaresque romances coexisted with novels of sensibility like *Pamela* and *Sir Charles Grandison*. In other words, just as people simultaneously owned (and probably read) such contrasting works as those of Cervantes and Scott, they also owned (and probably read) such opposites as Fielding and Richardson. See Winans, 'Bibliography and the Culture Historian: Notes on the Eighteenth-Century Novel,' in Joyce et al., *Printing and Society in Early America*, pp. 178, 184. Our point about simultaneous reading assumes, of course, that copies of *Don Quixote* or *Gil Blas*

Although less important than belles lettres, literature relating to the ancient world was well represented in our inventories, particularly in the large, itemized libraries. Histories of ancient Greece and Rome predominated, but there was also an abundance of works, sometimes in the original, by Greek and Roman authors like Xenophon and Ovid. In one respect, this is hardly surprising, for the idea that classical knowledge was the mark of an educated man had been strongly ingrained in Virginia since the days when George Sandys used interludes between the vicissitudes of the Jamestown settlement to complete his translation of Ovid's *Metamorphoses* and when William Byrd II scrupulously noted in his diary the number of pages of Greek and Latin he read each morning. Republican ideology of the eighteenth century drew innumerable lessons from the course of ancient empires and well into the nineteenth century an ability to make a proper reference to Medusa's cauldron could distinguish a public speaker. Yet, while it is a commonplace to observe that Virginians had a keen interest in the classics, it is the sort of commonplace that needs periodic restatement. Because interest in classical civilization was so enduring and because historians usually look for signs of change, we tend to forget the extent to which classical knowledge was cherished well into the nineteenth century. Further, the inventories testify to the extent to which such knowledge was popular, not an irrelevant body of rules and facts forced on callow youth by dour schoolmasters but a type of knowledge voluntarily acquired and earnestly augmented by individuals who were free to prefer other types of books.

---

or the *Adventures of Telemachus* found in Virginia libraries in the 1830s or 1840s were not century-old hand-me-downs that went unread generation after generation. Unfortunately, inventories do not show which edition of a book was owned. But it bears noting that all of these books went through large numbers of English and American editions after 1800. Mathew Carey, for example, published editions of the *Adventures of Telemachus* in 1806 and 1815; the National Union Catalogue lists nearly thirty English-language editions of that work between 1800 and 1850. Similarly, there were abundant English-language editions of *Gil Blas* and *Don Quixote* (many of them American) between 1800 and 1850.

While the classifications in table 5.0 give an idea of the breadth of subjects covered by books in Virginia's private libraries, they are at best cumbersome instruments for investigating the impact of intellectual movements, most notably the Enlightenment. In their study 'The Enlightened Reader in America,' David Lundberg and Henry F. May distinguished five categories of Enlightenment thought, ranging from the writings of latitudinarian divines like Archbishop Tillotson and Samuel Clarke to the corrosive skepticism of Hume, the Radical Whiggery of Price and Priestley, the still more radical speculations of Paine and Godwin, and the conservative rationalism of the Scottish common sense philosophers. Lundberg and May searched for evidence of the Enlightenment's impact in the catalogues of booksellers, library companies, institutional libraries (including colleges), circulating libraries, and a few private libraries. They found that by the 1790s the impact of the ideological ferment generated by Enlightenment thought was 'overwhelmingly clear.' The writings of Locke and Pope, popular before the Revolution, remained so. Addison, Montesquieu, and Hutcheson declined slightly in popularity, while Burgh, Price, and Priestley rose in popularity. Hume and Voltaire were in demand and Gibbon and Chesterfield maintained their 'immense' appeal.[43]

We found few echoes of this intellectual activity in the inventories. True, from time to time the Enlightenment all but leaped from the pages of men like John Thomson, a late eighteenth-century Petersburg political writer who, at his death in 1799 (at the age of 22), had a private library of nearly 400 volumes which reads like a catalogue of the Age of Reason— Condorcet, Price, Priestley, Hume, Locke, Godwin, Voltaire, and many others. But apart from Petersburg and Fredericksburg, one turns up few such nuggets; even within the cities, the impact of Enlightenment thought was mild, indeed ex-

---

[43] David Lundberg and Henry F. May, 'The Enlightened Reader in America,' *American Quarterly* 28(1976):262–71.

ceedingly mild unless one adopts the generous definition of the Enlightenment which Lundberg and May employ. They include, for example, Gibbon for *The Decline and Fall* and the French Jansenist Charles Rollin for his *Ancient History*. Gibbon was undoubtedly a representative of Enlightenment rationalism and Rollin's moralistic views of the decline of ancient empires endeared him to Radical Whigs. But the mere fact that an individual owned either or both works is slender evidence of the impact of Enlightenment rationalism, especially in view of the frequency of reference in our inventories to historical works (and particularly to works on antiquity) of almost any sort.

In one respect, Lundberg and May employ a restricted definition of the Enlightenment, for they confine themselves to European works and hence omit figures like Franklin and Jefferson who were unarguably men of the Enlightenment. Franklin's collected writings appeared in several of our inventories, which makes it impossible to learn which of Franklin's many views had an impact. By far the most frequently itemized work by Jefferson was his *Notes on the State of Virginia*. But even though Jefferson sought to answer some of the speculative criticisms of the New World made by the Comte de Buffon, his study was essentially a descriptive rather than speculative book.

Expanding our definition of the Enlightenment to include Franklin's *Works*, Jefferson's *Notes*, and such European works of doubtful relevance to the Enlightenment as Rollin's *Ancient History*, we are still left with the conclusion that the Enlightenment did not have a pervasive influence on Virginia's intellectual life. In Petersburg, for example, there was a total of seventy-four wholly or partially itemized libraries (excluding those in which the only itemized title was the Bible). Of these, seventeen contained authors associated with the Enlightenment, but, with the exception of John Thomson, who drank so deeply at the well of rationalism, and a physician, David

Walker, whose holdings included copies of Paine's *Rights of Man*, Godwin's *Political Justice*, and Hume's philosophical writings, most individuals who owned any books of the Enlightenment owned only two or three and these were usually works on the periphery rather than at the core of Enlightenment rationalism. Hume, for example, was much better represented by his uncontroversial historical writings than by his explosive epistemological writings. The same was true of the Scottish common sense philosopher and antagonist of Hume, Henry Home, Lord Kames, who was represented not by his philosophical writings but by *A Sketch of the History of Man*. Locke was an infrequent visitor to Petersburg libraries, and Rousseau and Voltaire were virtually unknown. If we subtract the historical writings of Hume, Gibbon, and Rollin, the number of libraries in Petersburg containing Enlightenment authors drops from seventeen to eleven. In Fredericksburg we found a similar pattern, with only ten out of sixty-six itemized libraries (nine discounting Rollin) containing Enlightenment authors. The counties revealed even less evidence of Enlightenment impact. Only in Fairfax did we find an appreciable number of private libraries with Enlightenment authors (eleven out of sixty-two itemized libraries), and even in that county only two men, George Mason and John Parke Custis, owned more than two books by Enlightenment authors. Elsewhere, it is difficult to find even traces of the Enlightenment. In Botetourt, for example, Enlightenment authors appeared in six of thirty-seven itemized libraries; however, if we omit works that might be considered part of the Enlightenment, such as Rollin's *Ancient History* and Jefferson's *Notes on the State of Virginia*, the figures drop to two.

One might conclude from this that the Enlightenment failed to make many strides into Virginia. This is true in regard to the more speculative and polemical documents of the Enlightenment. However, the term 'Enlightment' can embrace more than just the distinctive philosophical propositions of thinkers like Rousseau, Voltaire, Locke, or Hume. The term may also define a way of thinking that was more widely disseminated in the eighteenth century than in the seventeenth, specifically a fascination with the wonders of the visible rather than the invisible world. Given this broader definition of the Enlightenment, it is possible to describe Benjamin Franklin as a man of the Enlightenment not simply because of his deistical views of religion and Lockean views of government, but also because the most distinctive quality in Franklin was his relentless and insatiable curiosity about facts, whether those pertinent to history, public policy, lightning, or the origin of northeastern storms.

In this respect, Franklin exemplified what we call the working rather than the speculative or polemical Enlightenment, and it is this working Enlightenment which made broad incursions into post-Revolutionary Virginia. Evidence of this intellectual influence is reflected in the number of inventories that list books replete with knowledge of nature, such as Oliver Goldsmith's extremely popular *An History of the Earth and Animated Nature*. *Animated Nature* was a four-volume work published posthumously in 1774, and like many of Goldsmith's writings, it was a popularization of the more important (and more accurate) work of other eighteenth-century students of nature such as the Comte de Buffon. Restrained in tone, *Ani-* it was devoted to descriptions and classification of familiar and to provide the reader with 'innocent' amusement. Most of it was devoted to descriptions and classification of familiar plants and animals. 'It will fully answer my design,' Goldsmith wrote, 'if the reader, being already possessed of the nature of any animal, shall find here a short though satisfactory history of its habitudes, its subsistence, its manners, its friendships, and hostilities.'[44] Subdued as was its tone, *Animated Nature* was nevertheless extremely comprehensive, drawing on most of the sci-

---

[44] Oliver Goldsmith, *An History of the Earth and Animated Nature*, 4 vols. (London, 1822), 1:ix.

ences of the day. In this respect, it was similar to another work found in many Virginia inventories, one whose title can scarcely be called elliptical: *The Wonders of Nature and Art; being an account of whatever is most curious and remarkable throughout the world; whether relating to its animals, vegetables, minerals, volcano's, cataracts, hot and cold springs; and other parts of natural history; or to the buildings, manufactures, inventions, and discoveries of its inhabitants. The whole collected from the writings of the best historians, travellers, geographers, and philosophers* (London, 1750).

In addition to works like these, which specifically aimed to record and classify natural information, our inventories are replete with items that accomplished that same goal much less comprehensively and purposively. The inventories include maps, gazetteers, geographies, travellers' accounts, books on the anatomy of horses, and other aspects of the world of animate and inanimate objects. As noted, the inventories also contain many historical works. Writers such as Hume and Kames, most noted for their philosophical theories, were best represented in the inventories by their historical writings. The impulse behind this interest in history was probably similar to that behind the acquisition of natural knowledge; for history, broadly described, is a record of past facts. Some historical works, of course, seek to explain facts and to assign causes. Constantin François Volney's *The Ruins: or A Survey of the Revolutions of Empires*, written in the heat of the French Revolution, was informed by an unmistakably republican philosophy.[45] Rollin's studies of antiquity had a less clearly defined philosophy, but were scarcely devoid of explanations. Goldsmith's works on Greece and Rome, while indebted to Rollin, were less philosophical. All three historians were popular in Virginia. Without dismissing the possibility that Rollin's moralism and Volney's republicanism were appealing to some

---

[45] It should be added that Volney visited Jefferson at Monticello in 1796.

readers, we suspect that the widespread interest in history was part of a broader fascination with empirical knowledge.

This fascination with facts was partly aesthetic, for some facts were 'pleasing,' and partly utilitarian, for most facts were potentially useful. As the how-to-do-it category in table 5.0 indicates, Virginians owned many books that might be described as immediately useful: works on gardening, cooking, farming, insurance, bookkeeping, and navigation. The same can be said of the large numbers of estates that contained compilations of the laws of Virginia or of the United States (see the category on public documents in table 5.0). Yet it would be wrong to conclude from this that there was a conflict between knowledge that was immediately useful and that which was broad, comprehensive, or abstract. The conflicts between science and technology, or culture and utility, so intense by the late nineteenth century, had little if any relevance in our period. During the late eighteenth and early nineteenth centuries, few men perceived an antagonism between theory and practice. Rather, they followed Franklin in believing that virtually any fact about the visible world had a potential for public benefit. Our inventories reflect this by indicating that the more likely someone was to own Goldsmith's *Animated Nature* or *The Wonders of Nature and Art*, the more likely he was to own a book on insurance or law or navigation.

Although the speculative or polemical Enlightenment was poorly represented in post-Revolutionary Virginia's inventories, we need not suppose that Virginians were only interested in religious ideas. Our evidence merely indicates that few Virginians turned to books for controversial ideas. But many of them, particularly in the towns, did acquire large numbers of secular books. These Virginians became part of what we have termed 'book culture,' a type of culture that was decidedly narrower than that of print culture in general. Those engaged in book culture could share in aspects of the broader culture of print, but several features of the former made access to it more difficult than access to print culture and help to account for its continuing status as a minority culture. The most obvious difference between book culture and print culture was that books were more expensive than many other kinds of print such as newspapers. Less obvious, but probably more important in the long run, is the fact that book culture is apt to thrive only among readers with certain distinct attitudes. These include a disposition to seek kinds of knowledge relatively far removed from the reader's time and place. Books like Goldsmith's *Animated Nature* described not only familiar plants and animals but also those that readers were unlikely ever to see. Similarly, historical works described the rise and fall of long-gone civilizations rather than, like newspapers, the measures of the current administration. Even practical books like manuals on building often described exotic architectural styles. Further, books frequently sought to provide the sort of overview of a subject in its sundry relations that could rarely be gained from newspapers. The importance of gaining just such a wider perspective was a feature of Isaac Watts's advice to readers in his celebrated treatise *On the Improvement of the Mind* (owned by many Virginians in our survey) and of Thomas Jefferson's advice to his nephew Peter Carr.[46] This attitude was reflected in the frequent mention in our inventories of complete works or multivolume 'libraries' that purported to contain all that was needful for a knowledge of English literature or history. Not only did newspapers cost less and circulate more widely than books, but the reading of books was thought to require a far more demanding kind of intellectual regimen than did the reading of newspapers.[47]

[46] Watts's *On the Improvement of the Mind* was originally published in 1741. The key section, regardless of edition, is chapter 4, 'Of Books and Reading.' Jefferson's letter to Peter Carr, dated August 19, 1785, is printed in Julian Boyd, ed., *The Papers of Thomas Jefferson* 8(Princeton, 1953):407–8.

[47] While newspapers were more accessible than books, the per capita circulation of newspapers in the South in 1850 was only a third of that in the North. For further information, see Clement Eaton, *Freedom of Thought in the Old South* (Durham, N.C., 1940), p. 78. For a listing of Virginia newspapers before the 1820s, see Clarence S. Brigham, *History and Bibliography of American Newspapers, 1690–1820*, 2 vols. (Worcester, 1947), 1:1105–68.

IV

This study serves to emphasize the importance of towns in Virginia's literary culture. The literary culture of these towns resembled that which developed in New England towns during the late 1700s and early 1800s, and by the 1830s produced the popular dimension of the New England Renaissance, a dimension embodied less in the writings of Emerson and Longfellow than in the growing number of mutual improvement societies, debating clubs, and lyceums. The differences between the northern and southern incarnations of this emerging town literary culture were slight. Whether in Massachusetts or Virginia, the social groups from which its participants were drawn were much the same: professional men, shopkeepers, artisans, and women of literary inclination.[48] In both areas there were groups such as free blacks and unskilled white laborers that did not participate in the culture in a significant way; but the range of popular participation was, nonetheless, sufficiently broad to provide support for the contention of contemporaries that theirs was an age of reading. Further, the books read in the different sections were probably much the same. Books expounding natural knowledge or describing exotic peoples or places, as well as books on the ancient world and modern history, had a place beside the novels of Smollett and Scott, devotional manuals, and how-to books; all of these printed works taken together formed a common culture that transcended sectional differences.

Yet in the end we are led back to the predominantly non-bookish character of Virginia, for most Virginians did not live in towns. Even in 1830, after several decades of exponential growth, Petersburg, Fredericksburg, Richmond, Norfolk, and Lynchburg contained less than five percent of Virginia's population. In rural Virginia, where most people lived, there ap-

[48] Donald M. Scott, 'The Popular Lecture and the Creation of a Public in Mid-Nineteenth-Century America,' *Journal of American History* 66(1980):791–809.

pears to have been little dependence on books as a major source of ideas or information (save for the Bible). Even among wealthy planters there was no consistent development of book culture during the late eighteenth and early nineteenth centuries; and, unless we assume that a thriving book culture existed during the mid-eighteenth century and then disappeared by the end of the century, there was none in the earlier decades of this period. Outside the towns, the only group that displayed a consistent attachment to book culture were professional men. In sum, the sharp disjunction between town and countryside, which J. Mills Thornton and Harry L. Watson have shown to have been a characteristic of political culture in the antebellum South, was a mark of its literary culture as well.[49]

Was Virginia, then, an exception to the national trend of rising dependency on print culture during the early and mid-nineteenth century? The answer depends on whether that trend was, in fact, national. Contemporaries like Joseph Story who proclaimed that they were living amidst a revolution in reading were not only apt to gain their impressions of an expanding reading public from their experiences in towns and cities (where they spent most of their time), but they were also prone to let their ideology color their description. For such men believed not merely that the diffusion of knowledge by print was on the rise but that it *had* to rise if self-government was to work. It was probably no accident that calls for the diffusion of knowledge by libraries and lyceums became most intense during the 1820s and 1830s, a period when the democratization of politics was posing unprecedented challenges to the continuation of rule by gentlemen. The reality fell far short of the ideal proclaimed by these men. Indeed, the reality may not even have been moving in any consistent way toward the

[49] J. Mills Thornton, *Politics and Power in a Slave Society: Alabama, 1800–1860* (Baton Rouge, 1978); Harry L. Watson, *Jacksonian Politics and Community Conflict: The Emergence of the Second Party System in Cumberland County, North Carolina* (Baton Rouge, 1981).

ideal. Large parts of the country not only remained untouched by the appeals for an increase in book reading but may have been positively antithetical to such requests. Like some nineteenth-century missionaries who thought that the spread of Christianity depended merely on an ability to ship bibles to the heathen, advocates of the diffusion of knowledge underestimated the vitality of resistance to their pleas. They failed to take into account the existence of regional cultures in which factors like rural evangelicalism and (in the South) the code of honor enthroned an indifference that bordered on hostility to book culture. As late as 1934 a study of volumes per capita in public libraries revealed the continuation of what may be called New England exceptionalism, for not only the South but the entire Middle West and even New York ran well behind New England in such holdings; the proportion of volumes per capita in Pennsylvania was much closer to that of Virginia than to that of Massachusetts.[50] In view of this, it is probably misleading to think of Virginia or of the South in general as a pocket of resistance to an irresistible force. Virginia was no pocket or backwater. On the contrary, in 1810 Virginia was the largest state, containing almost as many people as all of New England, and was indeed the fount of migration to a different kind of West than the one New Englanders were trying to create.

[50] Wilson, *The Geography of Reading*, p. 99.

Table 1.0

NUMBER OF INVENTORIES STUDIED FOR EACH LOCATION

Petersburg	Fredericksburg	Allegbany	Botetourt	Charles City	Fairfax	Lunenburg
516	132	216	439	315	393	375

Table 1.1

NUMBER AND PERCENTAGE OF ALL INVENTORIES THAT RECORDED BOOKS

Total Number of Inventories Studied	Number Recording Books	Percent Recording Books
2,386	1,194	50.0

Table 1.2

NUMBER OF BOOK OWNERS FOR EACH LOCATION AND PERCENTAGE OF ALL INVENTORIES IN EACH LOCATION THAT RECORDED BOOKS

	Petersburg	Fredericksburg	Allegbany	Botetourt	Charles City	Fairfax	Lunenburg
Number of Book Owners	251	66	114	218	100	214	231
Owners as a Percentage of All Inventories in Each Location	48.6	50.0	52.8	49.7	31.7	54.5	61.6

Table 2.0

NUMBER OF INVENTORIES IN EACH LOCATION VALUED BY MONETARY BRACKETS*

	Petersburg	Fredericksburg	Alleghany	Botetourt	Charles City Co.	Fairfax	Lunenburg
$0–99	72	16	22	37	40	39	26
$100–499	128	28	77	123	86	99	64
$500–999	56	19	47	83	45	69	39
$1000–1999	70	23	20	67	39	50	70
$2000–2999	33	20	18	43	28	41	49
$3000–3999	29	5	8	30	14	19	26
$4000–4999	21	6	5	16	12	19	20
$5000–5999	22	3	6	16	15	12	15
$6000–6999	13	1	7	5	3	5	5
$7000–7999	13	—	2	4	2	6	1
$8000–8999	9	—	—	3	7	4	9
$9000–9999	11	4	1	1	1	1	9
$10,000 & up	39	6	4	11	23	19	30

* Note that the slight discrepancies between the numbers in table 2.0 and those of tables 1.0–1.2 result from the fact that some inventories, while they did or did not list books, merely recorded items without appraisal.

Table 2.1

PERCENTAGE OF INVENTORIES IN EACH LOCATION VALUED BY MONETARY BRACKETS

	Petersburg	Fredericksburg	Alleghany	Botetourt	Charles City Co.	Fairfax	Lunenburg
$0–99	14.0	12.2	10.2	8.4	12.7	10.2	7.2
$100–499	24.8	21.3	35.3	28.0	27.3	25.8	17.6
$500–999	10.9	14.5	21.7	18.9	14.3	18.0	10.7
$1000–1999	13.6	17.5	9.2	15.3	12.4	13.1	19.3
$2000–2999	6.4	15.3	8.3	9.8	8.9	10.7	13.4
$3000–3999	5.6	3.8	3.7	6.8	4.4	5.0	7.1
$4000–4999	4.1	4.6	2.3	3.6	3.8	5.0	5.5
$5000–5999	4.3	2.3	2.8	3.6	4.8	3.1	4.1
$6000–6999	2.5	.8	3.2	1.1	1.0	1.3	1.4
$7000–7999	2.5	0	.9	.9	.6	1.6	.3
$8000–8999	1.7	0	0	.7	2.2	1.0	2.5
$9000–9999	2.1	3.1	.4	.2	.3	.3	2.5
$10,000 & up	7.6	4.6	1.8	2.2	7.3	5.0	8.3

Table 2.2

PERCENTAGE OF INVENTORIES FOR EACH LOCATION AND IN EACH OF THE FOLLOWING MONETARY BRACKETS THAT RECORDED BOOKS

Assessed Value	Petersburg	Fredericksburg	Alleghany	Botetourt	Charles City Co.	Fairfax	Lunenburg	All Locations
*$0–99	25.0	37.5	45.4	10.8	12.5	30.1	19.2	24.4
$100–499	40.6	41.4	44.2	42.3	11.6	49.5	39.1	37.9
$500–999	44.6	55.0	46.8	56.6	44.4	60.1	48.7	52.1
$1000–1999	60.0	47.8	60.0	56.7	43.6	52.0	67.1	57.3
$2000–2999	57.6	44.4	77.7	65.1	39.2	53.6	75.5	60.4
$3000–3999	75.9	71.4	50.0	53.3	28.6	68.4	76.9	63.2
$4000–4999	42.9	100.0	60.0	56.3	41.7	57.9	85.0	59.4
$5000–5999	72.7	33.0	66.6	43.7	80.0	91.7	86.7	70.7
$6000–6999	61.5	–	85.7	80.0	33.3	60.0	80.0	64.1
$7000–7999	69.2	–	100.0	100.0	100.0	80.0	100.0	72.4
$8000–8999	33.3	75.0	–	66.6	57.1	50.0	88.8	59.4
$9000–9999	45.4	66.6	100.0	0	100.0	100.0	77.7	64.3
$10,000 & up	59.0	–	75.0	72.7	39.1	73.7	70.0	63.0

* We are assuming that the British pound during this period equals approximately $4.45 U.S.

Table 2.3

TOWNS VS. COUNTIES BY VALUE OF ESTATES

Percentage of Estates Evaluated at:	Petersburg and Fredericksburg	Five Counties
$1000 or more	50.5	48.0
$3000 or more	28.4	23.1
$5000 or more	18.8	12.3
$10,000 or more	6.9	5.0

Table 3.0

	Petersburg	Fredericksburg	Alleghany	Botetourt	Charles City Co.	Fairfax	Lunenburg
before 1801	53.3			43.5	47.3		
1801–1810	34.6	54.5			30.4	57.1	53.5
1811–1820	63.3	47.8		49.2	23.8	46.5	58.9
1821–1830	62.1	52.3	48.8	44.4	29.2		
1831–1840	43.5	48.4	68.4	54.1	26.6		
1841–1850	35.3		58.3	71.1	22.3		
1851–1860	43.0		44.4	52.2			
1861–1874			47.6	25.0			

Table 4.0

	Petersburg	Fredericksburg	Alleghany	Botetourt	Charles City	Fairfax	Lunenburg
Number	94 of 251	34 of 66	28 of 114	52 of 218	22 of 100	66 of 214	47 of 231
Percentage	37.4	51.5	24.6	23.9	22.0	30.8	20.3

Table 4.1

PERCENTAGE OF BOOKS FOR EACH LOCATION VALUED BY MONETARY BRACKETS

	Petersburg	Fredericksburg	Allegheny	Botetourt	Charles City Co.	Fairfax	Lunenburg
$0–2.99	32.2	34.4	43.0	46.3	42.7	50.7	51.1
$3–5.99	16.1	7.8	23.4	19.5	24.0	11.7	12.4
$6–9.99	4.7	10.9	6.5	8.3	6.3	7.0	15.1
$10–14	10.6	9.4	6.5	8.3	11.5	9.9	7.1
$15–19	3.8	6.3	4.7	4.9	4.2	3.3	2.2
$20–29	7.6	6.3	3.7	4.4	5.2	6.1	1.7
$30–39	5.5	3.1	2.1	1.9	1.0	1.9	2.2
$40–49	2.1	3.1	.9	.9	1.0	1.9	.4
$50–99	5.5	7.8	4.7	.9	4.2	4.3	3.5
$100–199	4.2	4.7	2.8	3.4	—	1.4	.9
$200–299	2.5	3.1	—	.4	—	—	—
$300–399	.4	1.6	—	—	—	—	—
$400–499	1.3	—	.9	.4	—	—	.9
$500 and up	3.3	1.6	—	—	—	1.9	1.3

Table 4.2

TOWNS VS. COUNTIES BY ESTIMATED VALUE OF BOOKS

	Petersburg	Fredericksburg	Allegbany	Botetourt	Charles City	Fairfax	Lunenburg
percent owning books valued at $20 or more	32.4	31.3	15.1	12.3	11.4	17.5	11.8
		32.3			12.4		
percent owning books valued at $50 or more	17.2	18.8	8.4	5.1	4.2	7.5	6.6
		17.7			5.9		

Table 5.0

PERCENTAGE DISTRIBUTION OF TITLES BY SUBJECT

(see table 5.1 for details of classification)

	Petersburg	Fredericksburg	Allegbany	Botetourt	Charles City	Fairfax	Lunenburg
Religion	15.4	23.0	24.1	42.7	40.5	27.1	41.1
Philosophy	1.7	3.0	3.6	1.7	–	2.3	.3
History, Biography, Memoirs	13.0	10.9	16.2	10.9	14.3	9.6	13.0
Laws	5.7	12.3	5.0	1.3	4.8	3.5	1.7
Public Documents	1.9	.8	1.4	1.3	9.5	.8	.7
Political Thought	3.9	2.5	1.4	1.3	2.4	2.7	.3
Classical Civilization	6.7	2.2	4.2	1.0	–	6.1	1.4
Belles-Lettres	16.0	22.2	7.6	10.3	4.8	15.1	9.6
Travel and Description	8.4	3.3	6.2	3.3	–	2.2	.3
Encyclopedias and World Books	1.6	.6	2.2	.7	2.4	.2	–
How-to Books	7.7	4.1	7.3	4.3	4.8	4.9	7.2
Dictionaries, Learning Books, Guides to Foreign Languages	7.9	5.4	8.7	9.3	4.8	7.9	15.1
Natural Science	1.9	1.0	1.4	.3	–	.9	.7
Medicine	1.6	3.3	1.4	4.3	2.4	11.1	8.1
Literary Journals	4.0	2.7	3.4	3.0	9.5	2.6	2.0
Music	.5	.2	.3	–	–	.4	.7
Almanacs	–	.2	.3	–	–	.4	–
Geographies and Atlases	1.9	2.1	5.3	4.3	–	2.1	2.7

Table 5.1

EXPLANATION OF CATEGORIES OF BOOKS IN TABLE 5.0

Religion: includes bibles, hymnals, sermons, devotional treatises, religious poetry such as Young's *Night Thoughts*, and religious history such as Flavius Josephus.

Philosophy: includes speculative works on moral philosophy, metaphysics, and epistemology.

History, biography, memoirs.

Laws: books about the law, books which interpret the law or tell people what the law is.*

Public documents: state and federal constitutions, statutes of Virginia.

Political thought: includes *Federalist Papers* and the writings of Locke and others on government.

Classical Greek and Roman Civilization: includes both modern works on the ancient world and writings of ancients.

Belles-lettres: includes poetry, fiction, essays, treatises on rhetoric.

Travel and description.

Encyclopedias and world books.

How-to-do-it books: includes works on gardening, carpentry, navigation, domestic medicine.

Dictionaries, spellers, arithmetics, grammars, including grammatical guides to foreign languages and French-English dictionaries.

Natural Science.

Medicine: does not include domestic medical treatises but works of the sort normally found in a physician's library, such as books on pathology, materia medica, therapeutics.*

Literary journals: includes *Spectator, Rambler.*

Music: non-religious sheets and books about music.

Almanacs.

Geographies, atlases.

* Table 5.0 is based on titles, not number of volumes. We made the decision to exclude law and medical books in the libraries of lawyers and doctors. Thus, the categories for law and medicine greatly understate the actual number and proportion of titles. Our purpose was to give the reader a sense of the extent to which non-professional men owned books on law and medicine, and also to avoid giving a misleading impression of the popularity of such books. While works on history, belles-lettres, and similar topics were more or less evenly distributed among our itemized estates, individual physicians and lawyers might own several hundred titles of medical or legal works in their professional libraries.

GAYLORD

PRINTED IN U.S.A.